I LOVE MY CITY

France Desmarais • Richard Adam

Illustrations
Yves Dumont

Translated by
Nicholas Aumais

pajamapress

Table of contents

All words marked with an asterisk (*) are explained in the glossary on page 55.

Introduction

The incredible history of cities is directly linked to the evolution of human civilization. Ever since their creation, cities have been places of extraordinary innovations. Most cultural, artistic, and technological creations were developed in cities. No surprise that cities have changed quite a bit through the years!

There are now many large metropolises all around the world. There are even megacities where tens of millions of people live! All of these huge cities have one thing in common: they are places where all kinds of people live in the same community and work together to create the best quality of life possible.

Cities are a place of great development in many different fields, such as industrial production, trade, construction, and travel using different means of transportation. These activities, which are essential to life in the city, also come with their share of problems for the environment. That's why many creative citizens are working hard to make sure their way of life doesn't contribute to climate change.

Through municipal democracy, citizens can express themselves and collectively consider how to develop safe and lively public spaces, and how to ensure access to different services that are essential to the community. Elected officials act as representatives for the citizens of their communities, voting on rules and laws that meet everyone's needs.

Understanding where cities come from, why they exist, and the different reasons humans gather to live in them helps us to appreciate them better. This book is an excellent introduction to understanding the origin of cities, their evolution, and how they work. It's also a great guide to better understand life in the city, and a valuable tool for civic education.

I hope you enjoy reading all there is to know about cities and discovering how wonderful they are!

François William Croteau
Urban Governance Specialist
Mayor of the Rosemont – La Petite-Patrie borough
(Montreal) from 2009 to 2021
Member of the Montreal Executive Committee from 2017 to 2021

How long have cities existed?

A long time ago, at the very beginning of humanity, human beings were **nomadic***, which means they were constantly moving to different places to hunt, fish, and find fruits to eat in order to survive. Over time, humans began domesticating animals and farming food crops. These agricultural activities led them to become **sedentary***. To protect crops and animals from predators and to defend themselves from thieves, humans lived in groups. That's how the very first cities were born! The oldest one, Jericho in Palestine, is more than 11,000 years old.

As you can see, cities have been around for quite some time. Thanks to archeological research, ancient cities have been discovered in places like China, Mesopotamia, and India. Each of these sites has been shown to be organized, with lots of distinctive elements that make up a city, like streets, wells, and houses that are joined together.

The ancient Egyptians had a **hieroglyph** to represent what they thought was the ideal city: a circle with a cross in it. The circle represents the protective walls of the city, and the cross represents the crossroads.

Where were the first cities built?

In the past, waterways were the best way to transport both people and goods from place to place. That's why cities were often built near rivers, seas, or oceans. Some rivers became important trade networks, which is why many cities were built along rivers such as the Amazon in Brazil, the Danube in eastern Europe, the Tiber in Italy, and the Ohio in the United States. Cities also appeared on the shores of seas like the Mediterranean Sea and the South China Sea.

Eventually, people began traveling by train, truck, car, and airplane. That's when cities started being built inland instead of near waterways.

Population

How many people live in cities?

Although cities have existed for thousands of years, it was in the 19th century, with the beginning of industrialization, that **urbanization*** took off and cities became more and more important. Rural populations began migrating to cities in search of work.

At the beginning of the 1900s, there were only ten or so cities in the whole world with a population greater than one million. Today, more than 5,000 cities have more than one million people living in them, but that's not all! More than 50 cities across our planet have populations over 10 million, and 15 cities have more than 20 million citizens living in them.

Today, 4.2 billion people—about 55% of the world's population—live in cities. This number will continue to grow: by 2050 it will double, which means almost 7 out of every 10 people in the world will live in urban areas.

How do you measure the population of a city?

A city is defined by its overall geographical territory, size, and population. However, to get a better idea of a city's influence, we must look into its density, which means calculating how many people live in one area, either a square mile or a square kilometer (km^2). Knowing the population density helps us to understand how the citizens are scattered across the city. It also influences the organization of services such as running water, sanitary services, public transportation, and more.

Shanghai (China) is one of the most populous cities in the world, with more than 27 million people living in a territory which measures 3,939 square miles (6,340 km^2). Its population density is 6,855 citizens for each square mile (4,268 citizens for each km^2). On the other hand, there are 9 million people living in the city of Dacca in Bangladesh, which is three times fewer than in Shanghai, but the city's population density is 47,368 citizens per square mile (29,000 citizens for each km^2). Since its overall territory is much smaller than Shanghai's (only 190 square miles, or 306 km^2) Dacca is one of the most densely populated cities in the world.

The United Nations (UN) has decided that a city must consist of at least 25,000 people, but each country has its own definition of what a city really is. It all depends on the total population of the country.

Canada is the second largest country in the world after Russia. However, only three Canadian cities have more than one million people living in them: Montreal, Toronto, and Vancouver.

There are all kinds of cities out there!

Megacities and supercities

A megacity is a kind of city where 10 million or more people live. Asia has more megacities than anywhere else in the word. Tokyo (Japan), Seoul (South Korea), Shanghai (China), and Delhi (India) are all megacities.

A supercity, also known as a megalopolis, regroups several different cities when they grow so big that their borders merge together. In the United States, Los Angeles and the Boston-Washington corridor (also known as the Northeast Corridor or BosWash) are both supercities, as is Tokyo-Yokohama in Japan.

Capital or metropolis?

So the number of people living in a municipality determines whether it is a city or a megacity. But the role that city plays in a country can give it another kind of status. Some cities are designated as the capital of a country, where the seat of its government is located. Ottawa is the capital of Canada, Washington, D.C. is the capital of the United States, and Ankara is the capital of Turkey.

A metropolis is the economic and cultural center of a region. However, a metropolis isn't necessarily a capital—and a capital isn't always a metropolis. New York City is the metropolis of New York State, but the capital is Albany. On the other hand, Kinshasa is both the capital and the metropolis of the Democratic Republic of the Congo.

Do you know what the words **metropolis** and **megalopolis** have in common? They both end with the suffix *polis*, from the Greek word for city. Knowing the origin of words helps us to better understand their meaning.

Cities built from scratch

Some cities, like Versailles in France or Saint Petersburg in Russia, were built from scratch to satisfy the desires of a king. Other cities were built around industrial factories, mines, and plantations so that workers could live close by.

In 1928, the Ford company needed rubber to make its tires. Leaders of the company began operating a rubber plantation in Brazil and founded a city named Fordlândia within the plantation where the workers would live. In 1945, the plantation was closed down and the city was abandoned.

The history of suburbs

At the end of the 19th century, some large cities encountered serious problems due to pollution and booming populations. To remedy this, urban planners designed **garden cities**. Situated just outside big cities, these garden cities had lots of room for green spaces and single-family houses.

The suburbs of today are modeled on garden cities. They are dominated by single-family houses surrounded by large lawns. But how did they develop so quickly? It was thanks to all the new ways to get around, including cars, subways, and buses. These innovative ways of traveling allowed people to live farther away from downtown or from the industrial areas of the city.

Nowadays, cities are coming up with plans to be greener and more environmentally conscientious, and suburbs are following suit. To reduce the impact of commuting, there are now commuter trains and, on roads, lanes reserved for buses, trams, and express shuttles. There are also many bike paths and walking paths. The main priorities are to improve access to businesses and public services, and to reduce urban sprawl by increasing population density.

A new kind of city

During the Second World War, bombs destroyed major parts of large cities. All over Europe and Japan, millions of people had to find another place to live. There were not enough houses for everyone. Government authorities had to quickly arrange for thousands of apartment buildings to be built in what became **new towns***. These new cities were planned and built in order to house thousands of people and offer them the services they needed to live well. In Paris (France), the community of Cergy-Pontoise is a great example of this type of urban planning. Stevenage (United Kingdom), Nova Cidade de Kilamba (Angola), Almere (the Netherlands), and Gropiusstadt (Germany) are also planned communities.

Favelas, slums, and shanty towns

The word "slum," similar to the terms "favela" and "shanty town," describes an area full of makeshift homes, usually built with recycled materials. Many people from the countryside who hope for a better life in the city settle there when they cannot afford to buy a house in the city. Slums are built wherever people can find the space, even on hillsides, near dumps, and in areas prone to flooding.

Very few people who live in slums legally own their homes, and they can be evicted at any moment. When and if they are available, public services such as clean water, schools, clinics, electricity, and sanitation are of very poor quality. The largest slum in the world is Orangi Town, situated near Karachi (Pakistan). More than 2.4 million people live there!

Ecodistricts and ecocities

Nowadays, we are more preoccupied than ever about the environment and climate change. That's why people are coming up with plans to create the most sustainable cities possible. These ecodistricts and ecocities promote ways of getting around that are active (cycling and walking) or collective (public transport). They also emphasize recycling, composting, and urban agriculture. Plenty of room is left for natural areas, parks, and playgrounds. New, energy-saving structures are designed to be built using as few resources as possible. Such ecological urban development projects can be seen in the districts of Bedzed in South London (United Kingdom) or Vesterbro in Copenhagen (Denmark).

A **demonym** is the name given to people who live in the same city, region, or country. For example, citizens of Copenhagen (Denmark) are called Copenhageners, while the locals of Niamey (Niger) are called Niaméyens.

How is a city organized?

City Hall, the city council, and public services

The city is governed by a **municipal government**. A mayor and a city council are elected by the locals. These elected city officials are supported by urban planners, architects, engineers, scientists, doctors, police, firefighters, and more. All of these city employees make up the **municipal civil service**.

But where does all the money come from to keep these services running? Some of it comes through municipal taxes, levies, and government grants. The city also has various sources of income, including water bills, fares for public transit, fees for building permits, and parking and speeding tickets.

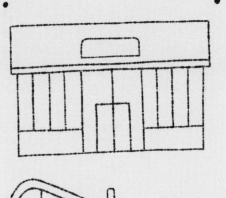

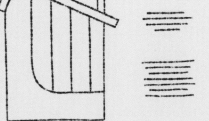

Planning and managing urban areas

Organizing a city takes a lot of work! Urban planners, engineers, architects, and the city council decide where and how each district of the community will be developed to meet the city's needs. Traditionally, the urban planning department **subdivides** the city into different neighborhoods, or zones, then assigns them specific purposes like residential (living), industrial (factories), or commercial (businesses). This is called **zoning** a city.

A factory might be built near a port or harbor, while schools, parks, and playgrounds will be built in more residential areas. The urban planning department will also work to locate the best places to build airports, train stations, stadiums, hospitals, and even theaters. Everything is carefully thought out, right down to the road networks that will keep traffic moving.

Not many people who live in cities have big yards. As with any non-renewable resource, we must be more careful than ever with how we use space. Cities must be planned in a way that limits urban sprawl and leaves lots of room for agriculture, forests, and other natural areas.

Cities must also adapt to the needs of their citizens. Today, the strict zoning of cities is being called into question. People want to be able to walk, bike, or take public transport from their homes to their workplaces, to shops, and to leisure activities. More and more, citizens are being consulted to better organize the neighborhoods and districts where they live.

FIRE STATION

CITY HALL

HOSPITAL

SCHOOL

POLICE STATION

STADIUM

Street name signs

To help people find their way across a city, street names are written on street name signs, also called odonymic signs (from the Greek *hodos*, which means "road," and *onuma*, which means "name").

Districts

The way a city develops is affected by the region's climate, geography, and available resources, but also by its residents' cultures and ways of life.

Two thousand years ago, **Roman military camps** were meticulously planned in a grid-like layout. In a way, those Roman camps are the ancestors of the residential blocks found in New York (United States), or the superblocks of Barcelona (Spain) and Brasília (Brazil).

The citizens of a city often group themselves together according to their needs, their common interests, and their commercial activities. In some cities, we find Chinese, Italian, or Armenian quarters. There is the Antwerp diamond district in Belgium, and a district of antique dealers in Paris (France). Cities all over the world have districts for business, entertainment, and museums, as well as historic districts.

Many cities have a Latin Quarter where colleges and universities used to be located, so called because Latin was the main language spoken by the professors and students of these institutions. Since the 1960s, several cities have seen the development of gay-friendly neighborhoods, where many activities and services dedicated to LGBTQ+ communities are offered.

Public services

Public services are created to serve the well-being of a district's local population: schools, parks, sports fields, public swimming pools, libraries, cultural centers, and fire and police stations. Public services also include facilities that exist for the good of entire cities or regions, such as hospitals, colleges and universities, and major cultural venues like theaters, concert halls, museums, stadiums, and arenas.

In the Wall!

In **Fermont**, a mining town located in the north of Quebec, Canada, all public services are grouped together inside a huge building which measures more than 0.6 miles (1.3 kilometers) long and 82 feet (25 meters) high. They call it...the Wall! The Wall contains a hotel, a hospital, an elementary school, a high school, shops, a sports center, the police station, and 440 housing units. This huge building is also a windscreen. Its purpose is to protect the rest of the city from the incredibly icy northern winds in winter.

LIBRARY

Safety

In cities, **public police and fire services** help municipal administrators accomplish their most important task: protecting the safety of citizens and property.

Police and firefighters are considered "first responders," so they must arrive as quickly as possible on the scene of any emergency. To help them do this, their stations are built in populated areas of each neighbourhood.

In the Middle Ages, **night watchmen** made rounds of city districts to make sure the citizens were safe. Each one would call out his own clever cry to remind locals to keep a close watch on their candles and fireplaces so that their homes wouldn't catch fire. Those watchmen were the very first of what we call "first responders" today.

C 9.1.1.

Services

A city is in charge of various public services, such as clean drinking water, waste management, public transportation, road maintenance, and more. These services may be provided by the municipality or by private companies. In either case, the city is responsible for ensuring the quality of the services offered.

Water is life

Water is a precious resource which is essential to life. Water—sometimes called "**blue gold**"—flows so easily from the tap that we forget where it comes from and how it gets all the way to our home.

Where does the water we drink come from?

Mainly from two distinct places: from **surface water**, such as a river, a lake, or a stream, or from a spring or a well that extracts **groundwater** from below the water table.

It's important to keep in mind that pumping large quantities of groundwater can come with some risks for a city. In fact, some cities around the world can no longer support the weight of their buildings due to excessive pumping. The northern part of the city of Jakarta in Indonesia sinks nearly 9 inches (25 centimeters) into the ground each year, which is a world record!

Access to drinking water

Another way to get drinking water is to desalinate seawater—that is, to remove the salt from seawater to make it drinkable. The desalination of seawater requires large facilities and consumes a lot of energy. Also, salt discharge into the sea often seriously impacts marine life. To this day, only 1% of drinking water in the world is produced this way.

How is water brought into the city?

Supplying a whole city with clean drinking water has always been a big challenge for engineers, and their solutions have varied based on available technologies, geography, and the volume of water they have to transport. They prefer to rely on **gravity***, meaning they collect water upstream in the mountains. That water is then redirected to flow naturally downstream toward the city. Simple, right?

But between the water source and the city, there may be mountains, valleys, and other obstacles, which is why **engineering structures*** are often necessary. The engineers dig tunnels and channels, and build dams, pumping stations and **aqueducts*** to carry large quantities of water.

How is water filtered and produced?

The water drawn from natural sources is not always safe to drink. Untreated water is often referred to as "**raw water**," and it must be filtered to make it drinkable. The filtration process varies in different cities around the world, but the goal stays the same everywhere: to make water clean and drinkable.

First step: **screening**. Raw water passes through screens in order to trap large objects that are suspended in the water, such as tree branches, leaves, and fish.

Second step: **settling**. After the screening process, small particles are still suspended in the water. So, the water is pumped into gigantic tubs where alum salt is added. The alum salt makes the small particles stick together and form flakes that can be disposed of in the city's sewers.

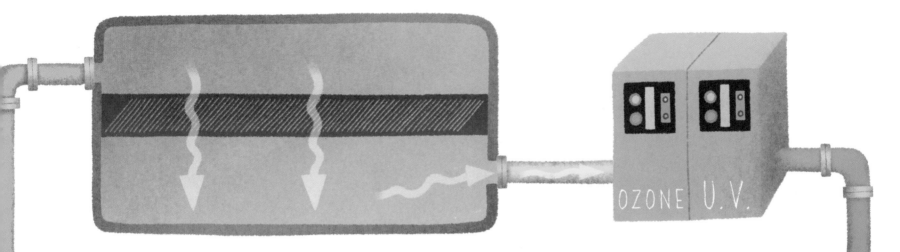

Third step: **filtration**. In another huge tub, the water passes through a bed of silica sand, which filters out 85% of bacteria and any remaining particles.

Fourth step: **ozonation**. Ozone is injected into the water to destroy any bacteria that might be left, along with any weird tastes or smells. The water is finally clean and drinkable!

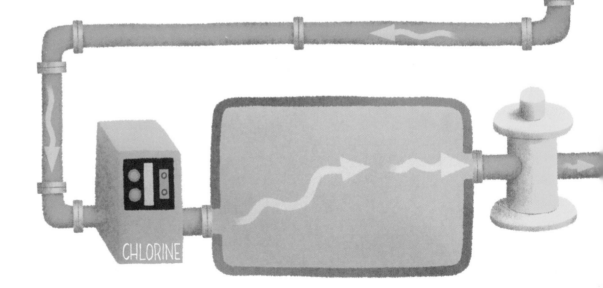

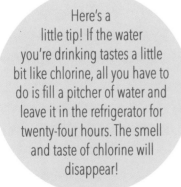

Here's a little tip! If the water you're drinking tastes a little bit like chlorine, all you have to do is fill a pitcher of water and leave it in the refrigerator for twenty-four hours. The smell and taste of chlorine will disappear!

Fifth step: **chlorination**. A small dose of chlorine is added to the water before it is distributed. This step is necessary to keep the water drinkable as it passes through the distribution system.

How is drinking water stored and distributed?

Storage

Once the filtration process is complete, water is pumped from the filtration plant to the highest area of the city, where it is stored in **reservoirs**. If there isn't a natural area elevated enough to get good water pressure, a water tower is built with a large **storage tank** at its top.

In the center of the city of Montreal in Canada, Mount Royal is both a beautiful urban park and the city's main water tower. Over the years, six underground reservoirs have been built there at different altitudes. Can you believe they contain the equivalent of 161 Olympic swimming pools? Incredible!

The City of Montreal reached out to artist **Luc Melanson**, who is also an illustrator of many children's books, to create an original design to decorate every manhole cover in the city's sewer system.

VILLE DE MONTRÉAL · EAU POTABLE

Distribution of drinking water: from big to small!

Just as engineers rely on gravity to help bring water to a city, they also use it to help distribute that water to homes and businesses. The higher the reservoir is built, the stronger the water pressure will be throughout the distribution network. In order to maintain the same water pressure when supplying more remote districts, pumping stations are located at strategic points throughout the network. The same goes for very high buildings, where pumps make sure the pressure is powerful enough to reach the upper floors.

Water reaches our homes through an impressive network of underground pipes. The main pipes, which are 6 to 10 feet (2 to 3 meters) in diameter, go from the filtration plant to the reservoirs. After that, water moves through ever smaller pipes built right under the city's pavement. The narrowest pipe of all, just an inch or so wide, supplies the city's fire hydrants and our homes with clean drinking water.

To make maintenance of the pipes easier, **valves** are installed to turn off the city's water supply at different places along the network. Manholes, which give access to the sewers at points all over the city, are blocked with cast-iron covers.

What about wastewater?

To keep nature clean, dirty water goes through a **sanitation process** before being discharged into the environment. Wastewater and drinking water travel in opposite directions.

In each house, water arrives through the tap and leaves through drains in the bottom of sinks and bathtubs. The water then flows into a small pipe, which is connected to a larger one. Gravity draws water from this main drain to the city's **sewer** system under the streets.

Between the end of the 19th century and the first half of the 20th century, **the Cuyahoga River** in Cleveland (United States) was so polluted by industrial wastewater that it actually caught fire 13 times! The last incident happened in 1969, more than 50 years ago. At that point, the United States government intervened to clean up the river. Since then, the Cuyahoga River has become the National Park of the Cuyahoga Valley, a beautiful place for kayaking and fishing!

The weird journey of wastewater

Dirty water—wastewater—ends up in the city's main sewer system. Large pipes collect sewage from many streets, or even an entire neighborhood.

After that, sewage flows into a special outlet (also called an interceptor), which is a huge pipe buried deep underground. Some interceptors are more than eight feet (2.4 meters) across! From there, the wastewater travels to the sewage treatment plant…end of the road!

How to turn wastewater into clean water

As with drinking water, **purifying** wastewater is a complicated process. The number of steps might vary from city to city, but the general principles are the same.

First step: **screening**

Wastewater passes through a series of filters that trap solid matter of an inch or more (about 25mm), like plastic bags, leaves, styrofoam cups, and much more.

Second step: **grit removal**

Water settles in large sand-filled basins where it is filtered to remove any leftover particles. This solid material is then sent to a landfill.

Third step: **flocculation**

A product such as alum salt, aluminum salt, or potassium is added to the water. This "flocculant" helps any remaining particles join together to make larger flakes. These are then collected, wrung out, and compressed, transforming them into pancakes. Weird and unappetizing-looking pancakes, but they are quite useful! In fact, when these strange cakes are dried, they can be used as fuel for the sewage treatment plant. And the water, once it is analyzed, can be safely reintroduced into a natural environment.

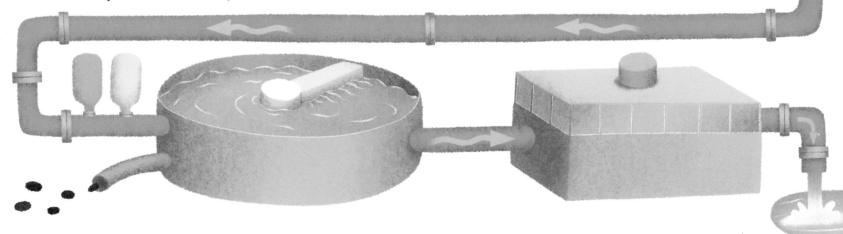

Wastewater treatment is relatively new. For quite a long time, sewer water—when there were any sewers in the city—was discharged directly into rivers, lakes, or even the ocean!

Energy keeps the city going!

Over the centuries, many cities were built near rivers for the sake of trade and the transportation of goods. **Hydropower**—that is, water power—was eventually used to operate the paddlewheels of mills and factories. Aside from human and animal power, hydropower was one of the first energy sources used to develop cities.

Energy is super important for many things! We need energy to cook, to heat and light our homes, to iron clothes, to travel around the city, and to do our work. Nowadays, because we're aware of the many consequences of **climate change**, we are learning to reduce the amount of energy we use, and we're turning toward renewable kinds of energy.

There are many sources of energy. In most cities, energy comes from **oil**, **natural gas**, **coal**, and **electricity**. These different forms of energy must be produced, transformed into a usable form, and transported into our homes. The distance between the place where this energy is produced and where it is used can be very short (as with solar panels on the roof of a house), or very long (as with oil or gas).

GASOLINE

29

Non-renewable energy

Oil, natural gas, and coal are not renewable forms of energy, and the impact they have on the environment is quite considerable! **Oil** is mainly used as fuel for cars, buses, planes, and ships, and even for heating huge buildings. Crude oil is found underground and under the sea. It has to be transported over long distances by pipelines or by giant tankers, then refined into gasoline or fuel oil, which is then stored in large reservoirs located in ports or near industrial areas. Gasoline is delivered by tank trucks to local gas stations. In the case of really big buildings that use oil for heat, including apartments, businesses, and factories, a tank truck transports fuel oil directly to users.

Natural gas, which has long been used for heating and cooking, is also being used more and more to fuel buses and trucks. Like oil, it is transported over long distances by pipelines, trains, or ships. In cities, an underground network of pipes delivers natural gas directly to homes, restaurants, and factories. When used as fuel for vehicles, natural gas is brought by truck to refueling stations that function like a gas station.

For a very long time, **coal** was our main source of energy. In many regions of the world, it is still used as fuel to produce electricity in thermal power stations. In some countries, coal is still used directly for heating and cooking in people's homes.

And, of course, we also use it to heat up the barbecue for a delicious meal!

COAL

Renewable energy

To preserve natural resources as much as possible, humans are increasingly choosing renewable energy sources, including **hydroelectricity**, **geothermal energy**, **solar energy**, and **wind power**. These forms of energy mainly produce electricity, which is used for heating, lighting, and powering plenty of domestic and industrial appliances—not to mention street lamps and traffic lights. Electric vehicles are also becoming more common, and charging stations for them are popping up along city streets and in parking lots.

Hydroelectricity is produced in huge hydroelectric power stations that are often located far from cities. Those metal pylons you see along highways support transmission lines that carry electricity from the power station to the city. Since it can't be stored, the city's electricity is produced continuously and distributed directly to buildings by aerial or underground cables. **Aerial cables** are what you see hanging on poles along city streets. However, in some areas, the **cables** are buried underground. Burying electrical cables reduces power outages, because they are protected from big storms and strong gusts of wind!

Newer kinds of environmentally friendly energy are also being adopted in urban areas: wind power, solar energy, and geothermal energy. **Wind power** generates electricity using the force of the wind. Have you ever seen wind turbines? They look like big metal flowers with three blades at the top that turn when the wind activates them…pretty much like a windmill. They are mainly found near the outskirts of cities and in the countryside.

There are also two kinds of **solar energy**. The first is heat, which the sun produces naturally. To take advantage of it, we can install big windows on the southern side of a house, where they'll let in the sun's warmth. In the second kind of solar energy, solar panels transform the sun's energy into electricity. Large ones are installed on the roofs of buildings, while smaller panels supply electricity to parking meters, parking terminals, self-service bike stations, and even road signs near schools.

Geothermal energy is another form of energy used for heating and cooling buildings, or even to produce electricity. Water pipes driven into the ground collect either heat or coolness that come naturally from the earth. In Iceland, where there are lots of volcanoes, geothermal energy is used to produce electricity and to heat nine out of every ten homes.

Connecting the city

A well-thought-out transportation network makes it easy to travel through a city's districts, and also between cities. As with the organization of neighborhoods, it's really important to make sure the network meets the needs of citizens and businesses alike.

Urban planners and **engineers** choose from several kinds of road, depending on the neighborhood: from residential streets to highways, to major commercial arteries, to attractive boulevards. They decide which direction the road will run, the number of lanes to build, and where to install road signs near schools, parks, and pedestrian crossings. Normally, streets in residential areas will only have one or two lanes of traffic, while a commercial artery will have several. The planners will also suggest the best places to build bike paths, and they will coordinate connections between subway lines, buses, and commuter trains.

Unique
ways to get around

The citizens of La Paz (Colombia) can get around using five **cable-car** lines installed across the city. In Valparaiso (Chile) and in Lyon (France), you can take a **funicular**—a kind of railway that moves people up and down a steep slope using two cars joined with one cable. In New York City (United States), a **ferry** travels back and forth between the boroughs of Staten Island and Manhattan twenty-four hours a day!

Traffic in the city

Individual means of transportations

To help pedestrians (people on foot) to get around, the city makes sure to have plenty of sidewalks and crosswalks. Pedestrian crossing lights are installed at intersections and near parks and walking trails. For bike lovers, some cities have built networks of bike paths and have installed bike racks and self-service bike rental stations, like BIXI in Montreal (Canada) or Medina Bike in Marrakech (Morocco). For those who drive motorized vehicles like cars, motorcycles, and scooters, the city makes sure its roads and parking lots are well maintained.

Public transportation

A city's size and its importance in business and financial matters usually affects the public transportation services it develops for its citizens.

These services must be planned carefully, taking into account the density of the population and whether the city is compact or sprawling. Subways and aboveground rail systems are both tricky to design, with their many stations and platforms. On top of that, there's the network of buses and streetcars that need frequent stops planned at specific places throughout the city, and commuter trains with their tracks and stations leading out to suburban areas. Cities must plan the many connections between all these means of transportation, so that a citizen can take a bus…to get to the subway…which will bring them to the commuter train…which will take them home.

What about shipping all our stuff?

The shipping of merchandise has a big impact in the city! Trucks and trains produce noise, vibrations, dust, and lots of pollution. To minimize these disruptions, cities impose specific routes for trucking and strict schedules for deliveries in certain neighborhoods. Recently, cargo bikes have become popular for delivering household goods. These funny-looking machines are a cross between a bicycle and a trailer. They are much smaller than trucks…and they don't pollute at all!

From here to there

To help them travel from one city to another, citizens can access highways, train and bus stations, ferry terminals, and impressive airports! All around a city's edges, clustered near the highways, you can find commercial warehouses, airplane hangars, train yards, and, in port towns, loading docks with giant cranes. For example, the John F. Kennedy International Airport located in New York City (United States) is a real challenge for urban planners. With its surface area of more than twelve square miles (20 km²), the airport and its activities have a direct impact on transportation, noise, and pollution.

Red, yellow, green!?

Traffic lights first appeared in London (United Kingdom) in 1868, long before there were any cars on the city's streets! They were needed to manage all the pedestrians and horses. The very first traffic lights were actually signs installed at the top of a pole. A person manually changed them from "stop" to "go."

Communication in the city

Communication networks are created to help people connect with each other. From smoke signals to carrier pigeons to the internet, communication is one of the fields that has evolved the fastest. New ways of communicating have even changed the way we interact with each other, since everything is now shared instantly.

A long time ago, when few people knew how to read or write, a **town crier** would read out public messages and announce weddings and deaths. But some communications had to travel from one town to another. In this case, **messengers** would travel by foot or by horse to deliver the news. In a way, they were the very first postal workers. Nowadays, you can go to the post office to have mail or parcels shipped, or drop them into a collection box. For most incoming mail and parcels, postal workers deliver directly to your home.

These days it's a common habit to read the news on tablets or smart phones. Even so, some cities still publish local newspapers, which are available at newsstands on the city's busiest streets.

The city of Paris (France) is known for its network of **Morris Columns**: large cylinders placed along major avenues which are used for advertisements. Many other cities use various structures for ads, tourist information, or sometimes community messages. A city can also authorize the installation of **neon signs** and giant advertising **billboards**. With their shapes, their size, and their colors, they make town centers a lively place. The bright billboards found in Times Square in New York City (United States) and in the Akihabara area in Tokyo (Japan) have made those places famous worldwide.

When color wins

From 1961 to 1989, a long, gray concrete wall divided the city of **Berlin** (Germany) into two distinct parts. Now that the city is reunited, nearly a mile of this wall (1.3 km) has been preserved and is used by artists. With 118 works of original art, the **East Side Gallery** has become the largest outdoor art gallery in the whole world.

THEATER CINEMA TH

PIM

BOUM BADA BOUM

Phone and **internet** services are provided by telecommunication companies—and cities make sure they use all the resources they need to build a fast and effective communications network.

To transmit **digital signals**, this network needs either wires, which are attached to telephone poles, or antennas. You can see large antennas at the very top of the CN tower in Toronto (Canada), on the Eiffel Tower in Paris (France), and on several skyscrapers in New York City (United States), including the Empire State Building. They are sometimes even found at the top of church steeples!

Some people install satellite dishes—which look like big saucers—in order to get a better signal. Whether they are attached to the roofs or walls of houses or hung on balconies, all of them are turned toward the sky.

Ecology, the environment, and sustainable development

Cities are growing rapidly. They bring together millions, sometimes even **tens of millions**, of citizens who produce billions of tons of waste per year. Food scraps are the most common; then comes paper and cardboard, plastic, glass, and metal…but don't forget all the electronic stuff, like old computer parts, phones, and video games! How can a city manage all this waste?

Not so long ago, cities buried waste in large landfill sites at the outskirts of the city. EVERYTHING was buried in these **landfills**, without any sorting. As a result, these sites quickly became full, and the soil was contaminated with all the chemicals that were dumped there.

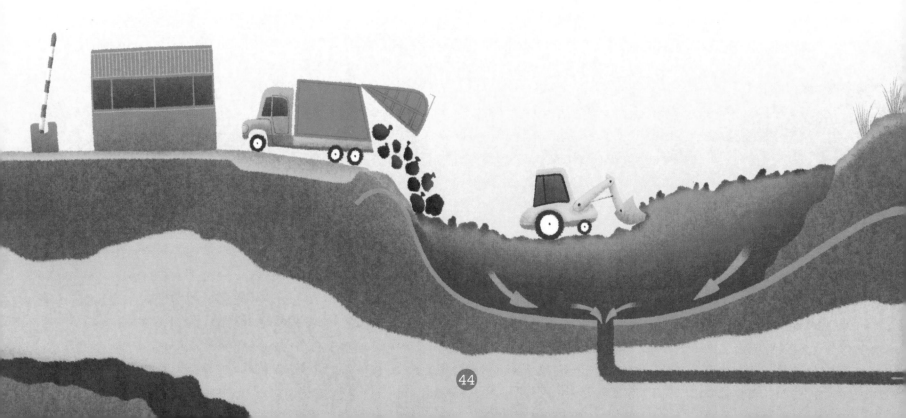

Nowadays, although landfills still exist, cities must find better ways to manage their waste, reduce their ecological footprint, and respect the environment as much as possible. To do so, they use the 3-R method: Reduce, Reuse, and Recycle. It's an environmental change that has to be made right away!

Existing landfill sites must be carefully managed so they don't contaminate the environment. In fact, good management can mean that, even at the landfill, not everything is wasted! Decomposing garbage produces methane gas, which we collect at the top of the **dump** and burn for energy. At the bottom of the dump, we collect and treat the **leachate**, which is a kind of liquid made of rainwater that has percolated (flowed) through the waste. In a way, you could call it garbage juice…gross!

Waste on wheels

If you wheel your garbage to the curb instead of lifting it, thank industrial designer **Charles Harrison** from Chicago (United States). His own experience with dyslexia inspired him to develop more than 700 easy-to-use products, including, in 1963, the wheeled plastic garbage bin.

The 3 Rs: Reduce, Reuse, Recycle

Rubbish, waste, garbage... While everything went into the trash in the past, that's no longer the case today. The management of waste disposal and recycling is an important part of a city's responsibility, and it's absolutely necessary to ensure public health by preventing the spread of diseases…and the presence of certain unwanted critters!

The Zabbalines

In **Manshiyat Naser**, a ward in the city of Cairo (Egypt), a group of 350,000 rag pickers—both grownups and children—live and work. They are called the "Zabaleen," an Arabic word that translates to "garbage people," although its modern meaning is closer to "garbage collector." The Zabaleen collect waste of all kinds, sorting out materials like glass, paper, and anything else that can be recycled. This dangerous work, which they perform without safety gear, is how they earn their living.

To encourage **recycling**, **reusing**, and **recovering** waste materials, cities have started to use "streamed" waste collection systems. In many cities, you can now find two or three **collection bins**. One is for organic matter, like food waste, the second is for recyclable materials, and the last is to dispose of whatever can't be recovered in any way. The stuff found in that bin will be buried in a landfill or burned in an **incinerator**. Several cities are actually aiming to be "zero waste". The goal is to completely eliminate the process of burying waste by reducing consumption, but also by recovering and recycling as many materials as possible.

A number of cities have drop-off points where citizens sort their own recyclable materials into special bins. There are also **eco centers**, which are places where you can dispose of old electronic devices or construction materials; these are then sorted and sent to recycling companies where they will be transformed into new products.

Green and blue spaces

Green spaces, whether large or small, are the lungs of a city, and they play an important role in improving its citizens' quality of life. They are also essential to the ecological transition for cities to become "greener."

In the 19th and 20th centuries, big cities began developing and managing large **urban parks** on their outskirts—parks such as Parque Tres de Febrero in Buenos Aires (Argentina), Arab League Park in Casablanca (Morocco), and Capultepec in Mexico City (Mexico). There are walking paths, ponds, bandstands, and even outdoor theaters all around these areas. Since the 1950s, neighborhood parks have been giving people access to playgrounds, sports equipment, and fields for baseball, football, and more.

Although large parks are very important, streets and alleys can also be made greener. Many cities have a growing number of pedestrian-only streets, **green alleys**, and resting places on street corners. Citizens are encouraged to get involved in their community by taking care of the plants and trees found in front of their homes. We can accomplish a lot if we consider every green space to be a space for **urban agriculture**. Gardens and green roofs are a growing trend, as are urban vegetable gardens found around houses and blossom-filled planter boxes on porches.

Water can be a source of fun. Citizens need a way to cool off on hot summer days, which is why you can find more and more public **swimming pools** and **splash pads** in many cities. Some seaside cities have natural **beaches**, but other cities build them from scratch. Even if you can't swim, these areas provide sandy beaches, parasols, and deckchairs. You'll find some of these pleasant summer escapes at Paris Beach in Paris (France), Dockland Beach in London (United Kingdom), and the Clock Tower Beach in Montreal (Canada).

A swimming pool that floats?!

In the city of Paris (France), a swimming pool floats on the waters of the Seine. Since 2006, the Josephine-Baker public pool (which is named after a famous artist) has been moored at a quay right in the heart of the city. The 82-foot (25 m) swimming pool and a paddling pool are both built into a giant floating barge.

Architecture and culture

Part of a city's role is to **preserve** and **refurbish** existing buildings to keep them usable. Tearing down fewer buildings means less waste—not to mention honoring the historical importance of constructions that have silently witnessed the evolution of the city around them. That's why the city's elected officials work with architects, urban planners, historians, and engineers to protect and highlight valuable community buildings. They also consult with the public and with specialized organizations to find the best ways to use them.

No one city is like another. Dubrovnik (Croatia) is not like Dubai (United Arab Emirates), and Brasília (Brazil) is not like Havana (Cuba). To better understand the historical evolution of cities, you have to look carefully at the architecture of their buildings. Whether ancient or modern, monumental, or **vernacular***, architecture makes each city unique. In the oldest parts of a city, you can find **historical districts** with their original monuments: cathedrals, castles, fortifications, or centuries-old houses! In a city's **business center**, the architecture is often more modern with skyscrapers and buildings made from concrete, glass, and steel.

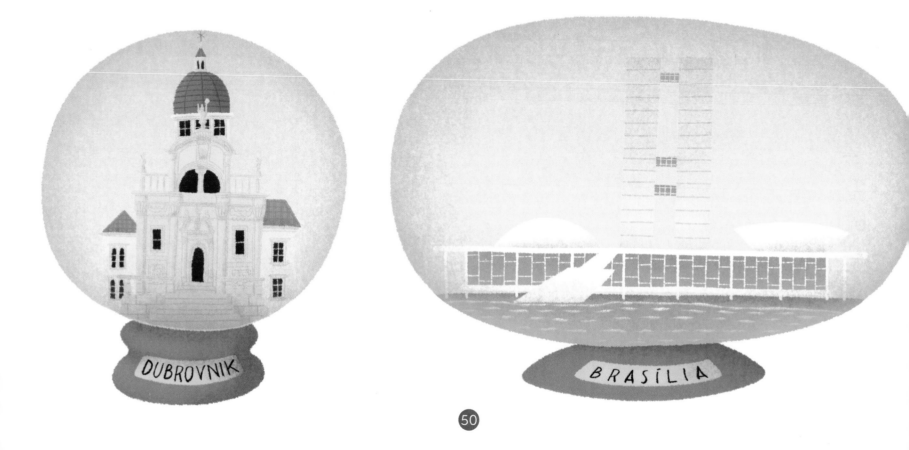

DUBROVNIK

BRASÍLIA

50

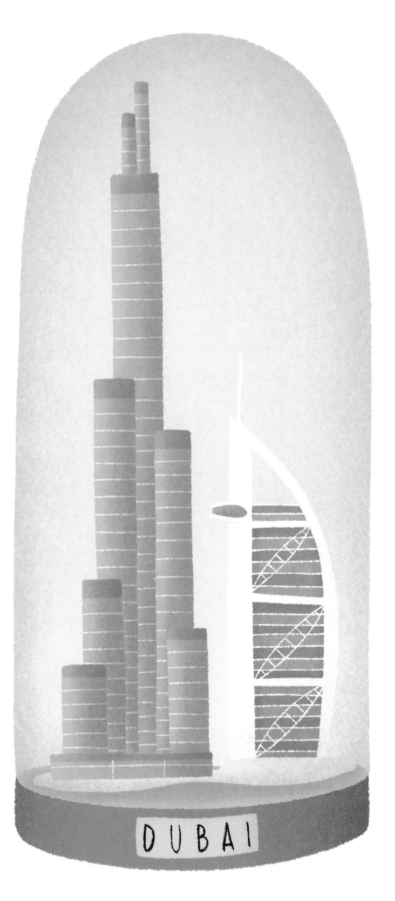

DUBAI

HAVANA

A gold mine of history

The largest coal mine in the world, which was also one of the main collieries of Europe, closed in 1986. Located in Essen (Germany), the **De Zollverein coal mine** industrial complex has been listed as a UNESCO World Heritage Site since 2001.

The mine's headframes and the furnaces of the coking plant have been transformed into museums, gardens, and hiking trails. The site also includes offices, restaurants, sidewalk cafes, and even a swimming pool in summer and a skating rink in winter.

Culture in the city

Most large cities have a department of **cultural affairs** that offers inexpensive or free cultural activities. With all the public works of art, murals, and other art installations around a city, you could say that the whole thing is one big outdoor museum! During the summer, in city parks, you can see a movie under the stars, attend an outdoor concert, enjoy a puppet show, or maybe watch a traveling theater group perform. And of course there's no shortage of artists and musicians who bring life to parks, streets, and public squares.

Theaters on a roll

Since 1947, an unusual vehicle has been traveling through the parks of New York City (United States): the CityParks PuppetMobile, which gives free performances and puppet-making workshops in all sorts of public spaces. In 1953, another **traveling theater** appeared in Montreal (Canada). Through the *Théâtre la Roulotte*, young actors put on plays to entertain children and families for free in different parts of the city every summer.

UNDERWATER ODYSSEY

"Culture" in a city also means libraries, cultural centers, museums, theaters, concert halls, and opera houses. These buildings are often designed by renowned architects, and some are so remarkable that they have become architectural icons, like the Sydney Opera House (Australia), the Guggenheim Museum in Bilbao (Spain), or the Bibliotheca Alexandrina in Alexandria (Egypt). Other symbolic buildings allow us to quickly identify a city: the Eiffel Tower in Paris (France), St. Mark's Square in Venice (Italy), the White House in Washington, D.C. (United States), Buckingham Palace in London (United Kingdom), and the Château Frontenac in Quebec City (Canada).

Conclusion

Cities are beautiful! And the best way to discover them is by foot. Taking a walk through a city district is like opening a big book. It's full of the great adventure that is human life, combining geography, history, science and technology, and arts and culture. Above all, the city is a lively place where many diverse people live and work.

The location of the city, its architecture, its urban planning…all of these provide valuable information that allows us to understand its evolution. The streets, bridges, docks, stations, and factories provide information about how the city operates, and about its economy and development. The city's housing, public markets, businesses, and parks can give us a pretty good understanding about its citizens' way of life.

If we want to make sure that cities have a bright future and continue to improve the quality of life of the people who live in them, it is our duty as citizens to actively get involved in our communities. Throughout the ages, humans have shaped cities in their own image, according to the values of the time. Today we need to make sure they reflect our values of inclusion, sustainable development, and neighborliness. While being open to the world, cities must respect the environment, protect their heritage, and make culture accessible to all.

To love the city is to love the place where half of humanity lives!

Glossary

- **AQUEDUCT:** an aboveground or underground channel used to direct water from a natural source to a city
- **GRAVITY:** a force that attracts objects to earth. An apple falls downward from the branch of a tree to the ground, and water flows from upstream to downstream
- **NOMADIC:** an adjective describing a group of people that do not live in one single place, but move with the seasons, or otherwise, to sustain their needs
- **ENGINEERING STRUCTURES:** very big constructions that connect two places, such as bridges, channels, tunnels, or aqueducts
- **SEDENTARY:** an adjective describing a group of people who live together in a settled environment where everything is organized to meet their needs
- **URBANIZATION:** the increase in population, activities, and services in cities and urban areas. Urban planning is the science of organizing cities' physical space and planning their layout
- **VERNACULAR ARCHITECTURE:** buildings that use methods and materials specific to a country, region, or era
- **NEW TOWN:** a city planned and created by a government or an independent company

Further resources

About how cities are developing:

https://www.worldbank.org/en/topic/urbandevelopment

https://www.un.org/sustainabledevelopment/cities

About water:

https://letstalkscience.ca/educational-resources/backgrounders/water-treatment

https://en.unesco.org/themes/education/sdgs/material/06

About energy:

https://www.pbslearningmedia.org/resource/nsn11.sci.engin.systems.smartgrid/smart-power-grid

https://www.sciencejournalforkids.org/key-word/renewable-energy

About recycling:

https://www.arte.tv/en/videos/100699-000-A/arte-reportage

https://thekidshouldseethis.com/post/recycle-video-for-kids

For teaching materials specific to *I Love My City*, visit: https://www.pajamapress.ca/book/i_love_my_city

First published in Canada and the United States in 2023

Text copyright © 2023 France Desmarais & Richard Adam
Illustration copyright © 2023 Yves Dumont
This edition copyright © 2023 Pajama Press Inc.
Translated from French by Nicholas Aumais
Originally published in French by éditions de l'Isatis

10 9 8 7 6 5 4 3 2 1

www.pajamapress.ca   info@pajamapress.ca

The publisher gratefully acknowledges the support of the Canada Council for the Arts and the Ontario Arts Council for its publishing program. We acknowledge the financial support of the Government of Canada through the Canada Book Fund (CBF) for our publishing activities.

Library and Archives Canada Cataloguing in Publication
Title: I love my city / France Desmarais, Richard Adam ; illustrations by Yves Dumont ; translated by Nicholas Aumais.
Other titles: J'aime ma ville. English
Names: Desmarais, France, 1956- author. | Dumont, Yves, 1974- illustrator. | Aumais, Nicholas, 1982- translator.
Description: Translation of: J'aime ma ville.
Identifiers: Canadiana 20220402019 | ISBN 9781772782738 (hardcover) | 9781772782837 (softcover)
Classification: LCC HT152 .D4713 2023 | DDC j307.76—dc23

Publisher Cataloging-in-Publication Data (U.S.)
Names: Demarais, France, 1956-, author. | Adam, Richard, 1955-, author. | Dumont, Yves, 1974-, illustrator.
Title: I Love My City / France Demarais, Richard Adam, Yves Dumont.
Description: Toronto, Ontario Canada : Pajama Press, 2023. | Summary: "In this full-color illustrated nonfiction title, middle-grade readers learn the how and why of cities. Topics include infrastructure and urban planning, municipal governments, services like water and energy, and how population, demographics, and geography affect cities' development around the world. Includes a table of contents, glossary, and further resources"– Provided by publisher.
Identifiers: ISBN 978-1-77278-273-8 (hardback) | 978-1-77278-283-7 (softcover)
Subjects: LCSH: Cities and towns -- Juvenile literature. | Cities and towns – Growth -- Juvenile literature. | Urban ecology (Sociology) – Juvenile literature. | City dwellers – Juvenile literature. | BISAC: JUVENILE NONFICTION / Lifestyles / City & Town Life. | JUVENILE NONFICTION / Social Science / Politics & Government. | JUVENILE NONFICTION / Technology / How Things Work-Are Made
Classification: LCC HT152.D463 | DDC 307.76 – dc23

Original art created digitally

Manufactured in China by WKT Company

Pajama Press Inc.
11 Davies Avenue, Suite 103, Toronto, Ontario Canada, M4M 2A9

Distributed in Canada by UTP Distribution
5201 Dufferin Street Toronto, Ontario Canada, M3H 5T8

Distributed in the U.S. by Ingram Publisher Services
1 Ingram Blvd. La Vergne, TN 37086, USA